SILENT PRAYER

Be Still and Know That I am God

By

NEW WAY TODAY

ISBN-13: 978-1511546935
ISBN-10: 151154693X

Author website information:
www.newwaytoday.net
www.facebook.com/NewWayToday

To all who wish to come to the water,

to the source of life,

to rivers of grace and peace.

To those who seek The Light Of The World.

To those who need shelter from the storm.

To those in need of healing and hope.

To those who long to know God.

To those who desire a personal relationship with Him.

To those whose hearts know that there is something more.

To those whose souls long for stillness ...

Come to the quiet.

Contents

INTRODUCTION

The fruit of Silence is prayer.

The fruit of Prayer is faith.

The fruit of Faith is love.

The fruit of Love is service.

The fruit of Service is peace.

~ Mother Teresa

Where does it all begin? Within the quiet of our hearts, we find God. Within the breath of The Spirit, we find Him who made us. Within the whisper of our soul, God speaks. It all begins with silence. This book will introduce us to a form of prayer that is both practical and deeply spiritual. Silent prayer will change our lives as we allow God to transform us from the inside.

Maybe we've reached a place in our lives where we long for God in a new way. Our hearts are restless. We know there's more. We know we are not able to find it on our own power. We must have access to grace. So we come.

Led by the Spirit of Christ we respond to His call, *"Come to Me, all you who are weary and burdened, and I will give you rest. Take my yoke upon you and learn from me, for I am gentle and humble in heart, and you will find rest for your souls. For my yoke is easy and my burden is light"* (Matthew 11:28-30).

We go to Jesus. He is *"the way, the truth, and the life"* (John 14:6). Within the ordinary, stressful, or monotonous moments of our day, we stop. We come. We receive. But where, when, and how do we do this? What is silent prayer? What does it mean for us? How will it affect our lives? Or, will it? These are questions this book hopes to answer. The short answer to what we will need is time and disposition. In other words: a few minutes a day and a heart open to God.

These few minutes can range from five to fifteen minutes to start with. During this time, we give God permission to love us. We open the door, and let Him in. This is silent prayer. We don't need to make it too complicated. We simply spend time with the Lord. But it's worthwhile to learn what that means and how to apply it in our daily lives.

What's a few minutes a day worth? Well to the God of the present moment who created time, it's everything. In centering prayer it's quality more than quantity. There is no time in eternity and God is not confined to the hours of the day. We are. He is always there for us, but are we there for Him? Are we willing to give time to The One who made time?

God is not unreasonable. He understands our struggles and our responsibilities to others and to our own needs. He knows our time is precious, and that it can be difficult to find the time to pray. He will work with us. God is *for* us, not against us, and He wants this time together with us in prayer even more than we do. He will help us find those five minutes on a busy day to somehow, somewhere, stop, and listen.

He knows this is a learning process. We are at the start of our endeavor to pray in a quiet way, and He doesn't expect us to fall into a contemplative bliss for two hours. We're taking a step, a step in the right direction ... toward Him. We are getting our feet wet in the ocean of Mercy and Love, and God will gently guide us throughout the process.

I strongly encourage only a few minutes of silent prayer each day to start. Over time, this may change, and you will increase your prayer time. God Himself will put this desire in your heart. He is always calling us into deeper union with Him. But for the purpose of this book, which is simply an invitation to grace, we will focus on finding some time in our busy day to come to our Creator, and "*be still*" before Him, acknowledging that *He is God*, and we aren't (Psalm 46:10).

All prayer is good. Both vocal prayer and silent prayer allow us to connect with God. We are engaging in a conversation of heart with Him. As in all conversations, it's a two-way street. In scripture we hear our Lord say, "*ask and you shall receive*" (Matt 7:7) and we also hear Him say "*your Father knows what you need before you ask Him*" (Matt 6:8). These two scriptures do not contradict one another. They are both prayer. Each plays the role each should play in our quest for holiness. God is not trying to confuse us here. He's drawing us into a relationship with Him, and as in any relationship we both speak and listen. We converse with God in our hearts. We ask God, and God responds. We receive. We reach out to Love and it's reciprocated. God reaches out to us. Whether this occurs with or without words does not define whether it is or isn't prayer.

Quiet, intimate prayer is a beautiful way of growing in this relationship with God. It is not to take the place of any other form of good and holy prayer. It is to be added to it. Let's not put prayer in a box as if it's one thing. God has as many ways of reaching people as there are people. Our prayer life is to be developed, planted, and watered. With time, and with God's Light, it will then grow.

Silent prayer brings us to a fuller prayer life. It expands it. It makes our words come to life as the author of Life comes to us. It produces fruit that lasts. It opens our hearts to Christ, in a new way, a way in which we can leave our false self behind and still be loved. It's a hug from God, and it's well worth our time.

11

Let's take a minute to understand better what this book is and what it isn't. The purpose here is simply to introduce silent prayer into your life. Nothing more. It's all about the basics. It's an invitation to pray in a new way. The intent is to encourage you to seek the Lord in the quiet of your heart, with the right intention, and let God do the rest.

This book is not an historical perspective or explanation of contemplative prayer. We will not be discussing the roots of centering prayer, or the awesome writings of our great saints, or any such beautiful book that, without a doubt, leaves this one in the dust. The depth of centering prayer has been studied and commented upon by some of the most holy and insightful people who ever walked or talked on this earth and we have so much to learn from them. This book, however, is not an advanced course, but it is purposeful, practical, and worthwhile. Who doesn't want to be loved unconditionally? Well, in silent prayer we encounter unconditional Love, and give Him permission to love us in return.

We were created by Love for Love, and He lives within us. Within our hearts He resides and we have a means to find Him, in the quiet. This is worth learning more about, however simple its explanation. The goal set forth here is only to learn a little more about this way of praying, sitting quietly with the Lord. What it is, why we should do it, how we can do it, and what the benefits will be, are worth exploring.

There are many different levels of intimate prayer, as there are many different levels of intimacy. There are different words to describe intimate prayer: quiet, still, silent, reflective, meditative, interior, centering, contemplative, etc. Each descriptive word has its own definition but whatever you call it, this is prayer that opens up our hearts to a personal encounter with God. We come, we let go, and we allow Him to love us. It is through His Love that we will then change, find peace, and be made new.

There are ladders to this process and this book has high hopes of conveying only a step one appreciation of the value of silent prayer in our lives. But this first step is worth taking, because without it we can't take the next one.

The simplicity of silent prayer is not always easy to define. Silence is both prayer and a way of achieving prayer. As Mother Teresa puts it *"the fruit of silence is prayer."* The silence comes first. We approach God, and when we do, we are praying. But this is also *a way* of praying, so the act of being silent in company with God is both a prayer itself and the means by which we become more prayerful. In other words, we grow in this type of prayer. We enter into a prayerful relationship with God that will never end.

What is the goal of silent prayer? With a deeper appreciation of God's presence within us, paying a little more attention to His voice in our hearts, and embracing the Love He has for us, we can not only find inner peace but we can be transformed and prepared to do His Will, which is the whole point. Centering prayer should be focused on Jesus Christ and it should result in bringing His Love into the world. Prayer should produce an others-centered attitude and approach to life.

You may have seen many books on this topic in which centering prayer is described as an end in itself. It teaches that inner peace is the goal, whereas in its true practice, inner peace is a byproduct of centering prayer. The real goal is union with God, discerning His perfect plan for our lives, receiving the grace to act upon it, and therefore growing in holiness. Bottom line, to do God's Will. With that comes an indescribable inner peace as we encounter Christ, who gives His Peace to us as a free gift - not as a reward for praying right.

So who's invited to participate in this type of prayer? Who's encouraged to come to the Lord in this way? Well, did you catch the *"weary and burdened"* part? I would say that means all of us. God is the Father of all mankind, and through His Son Jesus Christ He invites everyone to come to His table and encounter Him as the loving and approachable Father He is. All are welcome.

So let's come. Let's come and worship the Lord. Let's come before the God who made us (Psalm 95:6). *"Fear not, little flock, for it is your Father's good pleasure to give you the Kingdom"* (John 12:32). Let's make a decision to make Jesus the Lord of our hearts and the core of our existence. Let's respond to the invitation of Christ, and open our hearts to The

15

One who made the human heart, who knows it well, who has one Himself. Jesus Christ is the living, breathing Heart of God, and He's knocking. He's asking us to open our hearts so that He can come in, and make everything new.

We have a God who longs to see our face, who believes in us, who would like to communicate His Love to us. We have a God who has a prayer, if you can imagine that. What a glorious thing, that God has revealed His personality to us in Scripture and over and over again He expresses a desire to be close with His people.

With humility we approach God. "*It was not you who chose Me, but I who chose you*" (John 15:16). Make no mistake, God Himself is the one calling us to enter into the silence of His heart, as we enter into the silence of ours. Let's make God our treasure, our hiding place, the center of our lives. Let's *seek first the Kingdom of God*, and let everything else fall into place (Matt 6:33). Open arms are waiting for us. Let's come to the quiet now, and pray.

Chapter 1

Come As You Are

You are loved. You are accepted. You are enough. Only in God do we find unconditional approval of our existence. Who we are, not what we do, determines our value. We enter into silent prayer with this knowledge and hopefully leave it with acceptance.

Do we really accept that God loves us? Do we believe it in our heart of hearts, or is it something that just sounds really nice. The good news, we don't have to have all the answers before we come into prayer. We just come.

God is our Father. He invites us to know Him in a deeper and more meaningful way. If the requirements beforehand were to understand His infinite love first, no one would approach Him. Not only does He accept us in prayer just as we are, He *has to* accept us as we are, or He would never hear from us. Imagine if He let our weaknesses and our sinfulness prevent us from approaching Him. God doesn't expect or even want perfect. He just wants you.

17

The problem is, we think we are what we *do* and then it becomes very difficult to approach God confidently. If we consider our value to be determined by an action or inaction of ours, we can't know God in the intimate way He desires. We would be wasting so much time trying to be perfect rather than being loved.

We're not perfect

We have been taught by the world to think of success in a way that is completely inconsistent with the Gospel, in a way that is completely inconsistent with unconditional love. Now here we are, trying to enter into the space of unconditional love through silent prayer, and it feels uncomfortable. Why? We're not used to being loved for *who* we are. I mean, don't we have to *do* something? Don't we have to *earn* it? What are we loved *for*? What did we do to *deserve* it? It will take time to unravel this way of thinking.

The world places conditions on our worth. Our value is dependent upon the opinions of others and mistakes are presented as tragedies. Nowhere do we find a space to be free from the threat of disapproval. Everywhere we turn, we are being compared to others, defined by our outward appearance and the judgments of other people's impressions of us.

It takes an awful lot of energy to "keep up" and be who we're "supposed to be" so that we don't get rejected. Over time this became our normal, and now it doesn't feel that way anymore. We are beginning to realize that there's more to us, and maybe there is more to everything.

God is our hiding place

"You are my hiding place, you will protect me from trouble" (Psalm 32:7). We can be ourselves with God. We are safe and we are free in the Heart of Christ. We are free to be the people we are, while hoping to be the people we will become.

There is no safer place than the merciful and Sacred Heart of Jesus. It is a safe haven, where we are not judged by our thoughts and feelings. Maybe we're not ready to believe that yet, but we should still come. Come to the Lord with this concern. Bring your heart before Him and let Him listen to it.

19

Silent prayer is the means by which we arrive at this secure arena of God's heart. We come to this place with confidence in His ability to Love us despite our sins. Tucked away in the wound of His most Sacred Heart, we find our home - the place where we can just "be" without any side effects. It is in this non-threatening environment of love that we are called to pray.

We won't be rejected

You're not a mistake. There is a purpose to you and a plan for your life. God knows how we get treated in the world, and He understands that we fear He will treat us in the same way. Rejection is painful, every time. Too often, even when trying our best, we still get misunderstood or dismissed by others. Within the Heart of God however, there is no such thing as being brushed aside.

In silent prayer, we are always accepted. Remember that we are loved for who we *are*, not what we do. We need to be healed of the guilt and shame that has kept us away from God for so long. He wants to free us from the grip than sin holds on our lives. He wants to set us free from everything that holds us back. He wants to forgive us our sins and give us the grace and strength to *sin no more* (John 8:11).

"But God demonstrates His own love for us in this: While we were still sinners, Christ died for us" (Romans 5:8). Whatever we do, let's not allow our sins to stop us from praying! This is a trick designed to keep us away from God. Thoughts of unworthiness, guilt or shame should never keep us away from Jesus, who never turns anyone away.

We are all sinners, every one of us. We are all in need of God's grace. None of us can save ourselves. We need Jesus and His Mercy. We should make use of the sacrament of reconciliation, confess to God, and come to Him again and again in prayer. He won't ever get tired of forgiving us. It's what He does. He died for us already knowing we were sinners.

There's nothing you know that God doesn't, and He already loves you. Let's approach Him, even in our sinfulness, asking for His grace and mercy in our lives, confident that we will receive it.

21

Of course all of us offend God at times by thought, word or deed (or *lack* of thought, word or deed), and we all have plenty of things we need to stop doing and behavior we should improve on. Sin is never acceptable, but God will always accept the sinner. It is through an encounter with Jesus Christ that we change. Let's keep our focus on Him and approach Him in prayer regardless of our circumstances.

Approach with confidence

God knows our human nature and how fragile our hearts are. It is in turning to Christ that we receive His healing graces of mercy. Through prayer God breathes new life into us.

> *"Therefore, since we have a great high priest who has ascended into Heaven, Jesus the Son of God, let us hold firmly to the faith we profess. For we do not have a high priest who is unable to empathize with our weaknesses, but we have one who has been tempted in every way, just as we are—yet He did not sin. Let us then approach God's throne of grace with confidence, so that we may receive mercy and find*

grace to help us in our time of need"
(Hebrews 4:14-16).

"Approach with confidence!" This is encouraging. We see here that we don't have to go through some timid approvals process before we come to sit with God in prayer time. He already knows we're sinners and still invites us. We don't have to be perfect.

Not only is God aware of our weaknesses, He also understands them. He knows all the reasons we feel what we feel and why we do what we do. He knows every hurt word ever spoken to us and every defense mechanism we use to make sure it doesn't happen again. He knows who we've forgiven and who we haven't. He knows every childhood memory that still lingers. He has been with us through all of it, and He is with us still.

Having confidence that God is good and loving all the time is what brings us to prayer. Knowing that He won't reject us allows us to deepen our prayer life and open up to Him more and more. Please don't think silent prayer is the same old thing over and over again. God is always calling us to trust in Him more that we have previously and we receive new graces each time we pray.

In silent prayer, we trust that God won't turn away from us, and so we are able to open up our hearts in order to *receive mercy and find grace to help us in our time of need.* Without God's unconditional acceptance of us we would never get anywhere in our prayer life.

Our False Self

The spiritual and practical value of silent prayer in our lives is beyond words. The mechanism by which we achieve it is the absence of noise, in the quiet of our hearts, presenting ourselves to God. But who do we really present?

In order for silent prayer to be effective we must take off the mask of our false self. We all know the mask being referred to here. We each have our own. We spend our days wearing it, and on occasion in prayer we forget to take it off. We come to God with the right disposition, saying all the right prayers, admitting our sinfulness, ready to turn our lives over to Him and live a life of obedience to His Will, but we are not ready or willing to even give Him the mask. We pretend to be someone we're not. We fear rejection, even in prayer.

We think God won't notice us if we hide. If we could only grasp how much He loves us, mask and all, the mask would disappear. God is Love, and He can't be anything contrary to Love. It's His nature. He just loves us. It's what He does. It's who He is. We have a place to go to where our hearts are safe, and we don't have to disguise ourselves.

Our Real Self

We like to think that we define God, but really He defines us. We are who we are, because He is who He is. God is our Father. He came first, and we come from Him. You are a child of God, and your Heavenly Father loves you.

When we come to pray with The Lord, we are searching for both Him and for ourselves, since we are made in His image and likeness. We know we're in there somewhere. We are more than what we've been so far, we just need to discover it. So it's appropriate that we turn to God so He can shine His Light on the matter and help us to see our true selves more clearly.

"Yet you, Lord, are our Father. We are the clay, you are the potter. We are all the work of your hand" (Isaiah 64:8). If anyone knows the real us, it's our Maker. If we can't be ourselves with our Creator, who can we be ourselves with?

The depth of our existence in Love cannot be comprehended, and certainly can't be fully appreciated in five to fifteen minutes of prayer time. But as we continue to remain faithful to God in silent prayer, we will come to appreciate His Love and our purpose more fully each day.

A Loving Father

Let's ask God to communicate His real self to us as well. A tender and loving Father, who also has a desire to be loved, who wishes His children wanted something to do with Him. A God with a heart, who not only wants to be close to us but who also has the power to heal us and bring us into a new relationship with Him. *Through* Him, *with* Him, and *in* Him.

We need to let go of our old idea of an angry, harsh and punishing God who doesn't tolerate our humanity. We need to pray before we pray. We need to ask for the grace to receive grace. We can turn to God and ask Him for the grace to *want* to be transformed in prayer, to actually desire it. Let's ask God to reveal Himself to us in a new way, one in which we will want to pray more, and be comfortable being ourselves.

Let's look at God in a new light, and allow Him to come to us as He is, as we come to Him as we are. This is silent prayer: the act of just being together, knowing the other one knows. Without words, we let Love flow.

Hear the call, and come. Sit with the Lord a few minutes, heart to heart, just as you are. Don't worry about what you think or feel, just come into prayer, and keep coming back to prayer day after day. Begin with vocal prayer to start if you like and then just sit quietly a few minutes. Don't try to be perfect, just remain faithful to the process each day. God will take

27

care of the rest. He will bless your effort, and lead you in the right direction.

Allow yourself to be loved, without conditions. If we don't know how to do that, tell God we don't know how to do that. Be honest in prayer. But start the conversation with Him in whatever way you are able to at this time. God meets us where we are, and will guide us at our pace. What matters more is that we put aside that prayer time to show God we care about forming a relationship with Him. We show Him we want to live a life of prayer, a life where He is the center from now on. A life where He leads, and we follow. Come, and pray.

Chapter 2

Letting God Love Us

"Contemplative prayer in my opinion is nothing else than a close sharing between friends. It means taking time frequently to be alone with Him who we know loves us" (St. Teresa of Avila).

Intimate, meditative, and contemplative prayer has within it silent reflection. What makes it prayer is that we are conversing with God, we just aren't verbalizing our conversation. Our heart speaks to His heart, and He understands it. It is in the absence of noise that we are able to hear His voice, a voice that can be drowned out if we don't pay attention.

God is so good. He waits for us. Let's think about that. God Almighty, the Creator of Heaven and earth, the Alpha and the Omega, waits ... for us. It's really remarkable. God gives us free will. He won't scream and shout His way into our life. He gives us the choice to accept Him or reject Him. God respects our freedom. Love is not love if it is forced on us. God is

29

Love and He extends an open hand to us, but it's up to us to decide to take it. It's the hand that made us, and we have nothing to fear.

Our Creator loves us. He's always there inviting us, calling us to a deeper friendship and a more real experience of Him as Lord of our lives. But He can't make us approach Him in silent prayer. He won't turn off the television for us. It's up to us to seek out the whisper within, the Heart of our heart.

The bottom line in silent prayer is this: In God's presence, we let Him Love us. This is really the gist of quiet prayer. We are, and He is. We accept one another, just the way we are. We, with our faults and sins, and God, with His infinite His Love and Mercy.

Through this encounter, a wonderful thing happens. We change. Over time, healing occurs and things become clearer. We begin to love God more. We begin to love ourselves more. We begin to love others more. We more easily forgive. Our relationships improve. When we let go of our words, we begin to speak with our actions. We begin living the Christian life as we should. Our new way of praying, being silent in the presence of God, will actually speak volumes in our lives. We become better people as we allow Love to work in us.

"If today you hear His voice ..."

"If today you hear His voice, harden not your hearts" (Hebrews 3:7-8). At times, we have to admit, we're a tough nut to crack, and God isn't going to take a sledgehammer and break us open. He will, however, with our permission, gently melt away our outer shell over time, with the fire of His Love. We think this shell is there to protect us, but really it prevents us from becoming the person we were created to be and knowing God's Love more deeply, in a real and personal way.

Building a wall around ourselves closes the door to Christ. But again, God is so good. He accepts us, wall and all. We come into silent prayer with our wall, with our shell, with our defense mechanisms, and our hesitation. We bring all this to God, who alone can melt our hearts, and we let it simmer in His Love. Our protective shell should never prevent us from coming to prayer because it is only through the healing touch of Christ that we can be free of it.

Our hearts may be hardened for many reasons, some of which may be very serious and very painful. Quiet time in prayer may reveal what needs healing in our lives and what needs forgiveness. We may have unresolved situations of heart that need to be tended to so that Love can reign there and peace can enter.

Painful memories, regrets, fears, and even anger we won't admit to will not get in the way of God's Love for us. When these feelings and memories arise, we must simply remember that all our Lord is asking of us is that we stay with Him and continue to remain faithful to our prayer time each day, even if we bring these emotions with us. In fact, *especially* if we bring these emotions with us. Prayer may not always feel good, and The Light of Christ may reveal certain areas of our hearts that are broken, but it is this same Light that will heal the matter and make us whole.

We don't bring *some* of our self to God in prayer. We bring *everything* about us. We don't just bring some areas of our lives to Him. We bring all of it. As complicated as we are, God understands us. He really is the only one who does, and we have been told throughout

Scripture again and again, that He loves us. Our story won't surprise Him. He already knows all about our struggles and our weaknesses, and He loves us still.

Letting go of perfect

It may take some time to become comfortable with unconditional Love, as it is not our norm to be loved without having to do anything to earn it, without having to be perfect. This is true for all of us. I can remember a priest who once said, "*You're an imperfect person, living among other imperfect people, in an imperfect world. Ask yourself if you can you live with that.*" What He was really saying was nobody's perfect, this is life, God knows it, accept it and be at peace. God knew I needed to hear that. I know it sounds obvious but it was a significant way of putting it.

Of course I'm not perfect and I have no right to expect perfection from others either. I knew this in my mind but it wasn't so easy to do in my heart since I was still demanding perfection from myself in my prayer life. It took time to accept that I am *always* imperfect in God's presence and His Love doesn't take my imperfections into consideration. He just loves me. I couldn't earn it if I tried. Being imperfect or even being perfect wouldn't make Him love me less or more. Love is His natural state. It's who He is and what He does. I don't change that.

What silent prayer is ...

In silent prayer, we give to God and God gives to us. What do we give Him? Ourselves. What does He give us? Himself. We give Him our time and make a commitment to spend a certain amount of it each and every day with Him in prayer. We give Him a place, both a physical place of quiet and a place in our hearts with the right disposition of allowing Him to enter. We give Him our words, trusting that He already knows our situation and wants to simply flood it with His Light.

It may be easy to use this five to fifteen minutes of prayer time to explain our current situation to Him, going over every detail, making sure He understands and knows the whole story, and doesn't miss any of the fine points, but that wouldn't leave much time for anything else. Not to mention, we would be controlling the encounter, and in silent prayer we let go of control and place this precious time in His hands.

That's not to say that we can't take some extra time and begin with vocal prayer or reading scripture. Talking with God is not a lesser form of prayer, and it's actually a nice introduction before we begin quiet prayer, especially if we're new at this. But our topic is silent prayer and such prayer begins by setting aside some quiet time and saying to the Lord, "these next few minutes are completely for you." We turn off the television, the cell phone, the games, the computer and put away the magazines and "to do" lists. We choose to be quiet, and then sit there. Under the surface, it's deeper than that, but this is where we begin.

We sit with the Lord, with faith that He is with us. We may or may not feel His presence, but we come anyway and spend a few minutes in stillness, safe and sound, with an open heart. Then we do it again tomorrow, and the day after that. Soon we will notice some really positive changes occurring. We will be able to quiet our mind more easily. We will become more peaceful, and less likely to react to things too quickly. We will be more patient. We will become calmer and start caring more about the things of God.

What matters most is the quality of the time spent and our faithfulness to it. We don't allow our feelings to determine whether or not this type of prayer is useful. It's not a quick fix. It's spiritual growth, and growth takes time. The word growth is defined as, "*the act or process, or manner of growing; a stage; a process of development; or gradual increase.*" Nothing in this language sounds fast.

We make a decision whether or not to give God our time, actually whether or not to give Him back some of the time He gave us. We give some time and space to The One who created time and space. We let The One who made our hearts, *live* in our hearts.

This is our free will in action, choosing God, responding yes to His invitation. The very act of saying to the Lord, "okay, I've taken everything else off my plate so that you and I can spend this time together" is no small thing. Just making the decision to grow in faith, is pleasing to the Lord. How we go about it are details that will get worked out. We just come. We show up. Our Lord will do the rest.

What silent prayer isn't ...

Silent prayer is not an end in itself. We are forming a relationship with our Creator, and as in any relationship we must spend time with the person. There is a starting point, but there is no end to our relationship with God.

When the world presents "spirituality" to us it usually does so in an effort to achieve one's own will, goals, and dreams ... and if it doesn't do that directly then it indirectly presupposes God's Will (in the form of one's own will, goals and dreams). It sounds lovely, and can be spun to sound holy, but it's inconsistent with God's Word.

This approach to spirituality is false. It doesn't make Jesus the center. It makes *us* the center. It's not prayer. It teaches that whatever we want is ok. It's claiming God to be who we want Him to be. It's making up a God for each of us based on our own desires, rather than entering into a process in which we will discover *His Will* for our lives as *He reveals Himself* to us through prayer.

Centering prayer, in its true practice, is never selfish. There is a great irony about the fact that solitude leads to a Christ-centered and others-centered dimension in our lives. You would think the opposite would occur. You would think the more we look within ourselves, the more we become consumed with ourselves. Instead, when it's done properly, in and with and through Christ, the process of looking within actually draws us out of ourselves. We are searching for God. We become *less* focused on ourselves and more focused on bringing the Love that we have found within us to others.

When we truly practice silent prayer, we encounter Jesus in our heart. When we meet Christ we change. That's just what happens when we cross paths with God. We don't stay the same. Something happens and our soul is moved, whether we are aware of it or not, and we are set on the right path. We are drawn into His presence by Love. He leads and we follow.

The world uses God as a tool, as a means to getting what we want out of life, rather than accepting that He *is* our life, the foundation on which we should build. Jesus Himself is *The Way, The Truth, and The Life* (John 14:6), and all forms of prayer that ignore this truth, even if they provide some temporary feeling of peace, will ultimately leave us empty. Jesus is not the question. He is the answer.

Through silent prayer, Jesus will help us to see our heart's desire more clearly. What we really want is *Him*. We maybe just don't know it yet. We want to be loved, and He can give us what we want. He already has the Love we long for. He *is* the Love we long for, and through prayer we will come to realize it. Silent prayer teaches us to follow God's voice in our lives, but we must take some time and turn off the noise of the world in order to hear it.

We take the step

It can't be emphasized enough how pleasing it is to God that we seek Him out. We have a God who waits for us, as only a God who has given us free will can, but so many don't come. So many of His children go about life as if they created themselves and don't have a maker. So many people who once believed in

God, have allowed suffering to lead them away rather than lead them closer to His arms. God waits in vain for so many to return to Him or to seek Him out. But He still waits. His arms are still open. Even if we leave Him, He never leaves us.

God doesn't owe us anything. The proof of His Love for us is already on the cross. Yet, He still desires to reveal Himself to us even more. He wants us to experience Him directly, personally. He's given us everything. As if His blood wasn't enough, He has given us His own Spirit through Baptism to live within us and help us to carry out His Will. In fact, it is The Holy Spirit, Love itself, who guides us in silent prayer. *"The Spirit of Truth, He will guide you to all Truth" (John 16:13).*

Silent prayer is practical, purposeful and spiritual. God is just a prayer away. But we can't pray effectively without Him. Without humbly accepting this fact, silent prayer will just be quiet time with ourselves.

Chapter 3

The Big Picture

"Here I am. I stand at the door and knock. If anyone hears my voice and opens the door, I will come in and eat with that person, and they with me" (Revelation 3:20).

What are we looking for? What are the reasons we want to enter into silent prayer? Our Lord is at the door of our hearts, and we're ready to open it for Him. What is our motivation for doing so? What mindset should we have when approaching God?

You might be familiar with the famous painting called "The Light of the World" by William Holman Hunt, painted again in various forms by other artists also. It's a beautiful painting with a deeply spiritual message than we can reflect on. In this painting, Jesus is standing at a door, knocking, wanting to come in, seeking permission. The door has no handle on the outside. It can only be opened from the inside. What is Jesus to do if no one opens it? Break it down and force His way in?

Our intentions toward God

We come into silent prayer to form a relationship with God and to receive the graces of that relationship. Wanting something from God is not selfish. If we have reached a point in our lives where we are seeking the Lord in a deeper form of prayer, the things we probably want are inner peace, grace, healing and wholeness.

We need strength for our day and calm in our hearts. We're tired, and we need rest. Rest for our body, our mind and our soul. We need answers to prayers for our loved ones who are struggling. We want God's guidance in our lives, or maybe, we just want a Divine hug. We want to be in the presence of our maker, safe and sound, hearing in our hearts that everything will be ok. We want to be loved.

In silent prayer we come to the right place to find these things. The Heart of Jesus is the source of all that is good, and these are all good and holy reasons to enter into silent prayer. God not only wants to give us the special graces we need in life, He is the only one who can. God alone can fill our hearts in the way they were created to be filled. We are the work of His hands. He knows what to do.

Maybe our intentions are practical. God desires to provide for us, and help us in our every day needs. It's ok to ask and it's ok to receive. He understands our humanity and is sensitive to all of our prayers.

Maybe our intentions are more spiritual. Perhaps we are in need of emotional healing. Maybe we're searching for the Lord for the first time and we're still struggling to believe in Him. We enter into silent prayer hoping to find Him, to experience Him, and to understand what people mean by a "personal relationship with Jesus Christ."

Or maybe our intentions go even deeper, desiring a closer union with God in prayer, desiring to surrender to Him and do His Will in all matters, looking to be renewed and refreshed by His grace.

With high hopes, or with skepticism, we come into quiet prayer wanting God to reveal Himself to us, to remind us that He is really there, and that He really does care about what's going on in our lives.

All prayer is good and our Lord wants us to communicate with Him, and turn to Him for our needs. We come into silent prayer with good intentions, with petitions of the heart that are beyond words.

God's intentions toward us

Why does God want to spend time with us? Well, believe it or not, for the same reasons we do - to form a relationship with us. He, however, knows how such a relationship will benefit us. He knows we were created to have this relationship with Him, and through it we will find our purpose.

Through intimate prayer we look for God and come to know Him as He really is, and in doing so we come to discover who we really are too. Since we are made in His image, we will see our reflection ... but only if we are looking.

God's intentions are pure. Our Creator wants to be with His creation. He can't separate Himself from what He has made. We are the work of His hands. He is always with us. We only have to realize it.

Centering prayer is where our intentions and God's intentions meet, and we just love one another. The goal of silent prayer has some basic elements but there are different levels. The ultimate goal is to achieve a state where there is no difference of intention at all. Our will becomes one with His Will. We will want what He wants and we will love as He Loves, just as He commanded us.

Let's not get discouraged if we're not there yet. Silent prayer deepens over time, but it begins by making a decision to start. By taking this first step we take a seat at the table where the Lord, as we read at the start of this chapter, will "*come in and eat with that person, and they with Me.*" At this point it's simply a get-together, a meeting place, where the *weary and burdened* are called to go, knowing that Christ will be there too.

Happiness and Holiness

God wants us to be with Him forever. He wants us to be Happy, not in the way the world does, quickly and temporarily, but eternally. As we draw closer to the Light of Christ in prayer, things will become clearer. We will begin to see that happiness cannot be found in people, places or things, but in God alone. When we enter into silent prayer we are seeking this place of Light, a place of grace that will transform us and make us new. The Happiness God offers us will last forever. This Happiness is achieved through Holiness.

Holiness is not perfection. Holiness is the act of trying again. *"But one thing I do, forgetting what lies behind and straining forward to what lies ahead, I press on toward the goal for the prize of the upward call of God in Christ Jesus"* (Phil 3:13-14).

It's when we persevere through our struggle in the spiritual life, and keep moving forward, despite opposition, that we will grow in Holiness. Prayer gives us the strength we need to get up and keep going.

Through prayer we receive everything we need to grow in Holiness, to grow closer to God. We look at Jesus, who fell three times on the road to Calvary but kept getting up, moving forward toward the Cross, and to The Resurrection. This gives us hope, and will free us from discouragement. In silent prayer, we encounter Him, The Holy One, who loves us just as we are, sinner and all, and encourages us to keep moving forward in Love. Through Him, we can achieve an eternal happiness.

There's a quiet place within you. And your soul knows it. It's a place where things are calm, where the waters are still, where the storm has left. It's a place where peace rules and life is precious. A place where you are understood and accepted. A place where you don't have to pretend, a place where you can find rest. Come to that place now. Come, and pray. Ask God to lead you to the water, and never be thirsty again.

Chapter 4

God Knows

"Lord, You have searched me and known me. You know when I sit down and when I stand up. You understand my thoughts from far away. You observe my travels and my rest. You are aware of all my ways. Before a word is on my tongue, You know all about it, Lord." (Psalm 139:1-6)

God knows we are sinners

Silent prayer isn't so much about the *what* as it is about the *who*. Yes, God knows everything about us. He knows all of the sins of our lives and He Loves us anyway. Our sinfulness will not surprise Him. Jesus already knows, and already loves us.

God doesn't want to remember our sins anymore (Isaiah 43:25). He is ready, willing and able to forgive our sins, and don't be deceived we are all in need of His forgiveness. Sin is real. We can and do offend God and we must call it what it is. But Jesus came to die, to take our sins upon Himself, in order to free us from sin. He knows how destructive it is to us, and to the people in our lives, and how easily it hurts us and keeps us from approaching Him. Jesus has the power to heal and repair our brokenness. He can make us new. So let's confess our sins and receive His grace and mercy and try again. We have a God of new beginnings. He will give us a clean slate and a fresh start, no matter what.

We should never allow our sinfulness to prevent us from praying. In fact, admitting our sinfulness in prayer is holy. This is exactly when we need God the most and when we turn to Him in prayer He will never turn us away.

The point is not that God knows our sins but that He loves us despite them. He really is, as the Psalm says, *The All-Knowing and Ever-Present God,* but it's not about what He knows as much as it's about His Love. God loves us, and there's nothing we can do about it.

God wants us to come to Him, words or no words. He just wants His children back. Please don't think that silent prayer is better than verbal prayer. All prayer is good. God loves when we talk to Him, when we reach up as children do to their parent and tell Him all about our day. He wants that. He loves to hear our words because it means we're communicating with Him which is the basis for having a relationship. But He also wants our heart.

In conversing with God we are building a foundation for our life. But when we do all the talking in prayer, how can we listen? Some silent time with an open heart will help us to discern God's voice in our lives a little more clearly.

God knows our heart

God knows everything in our life that has led us here. He knows every scrape and cut. He knows every wound and want. He knows every anxious thought and painful memory. He knows every tear that has fallen from our eyes, and He knows we think He could have prevented them.

We sometimes put on a pretty face when we come to prayer time, when truthfully we are angry or disappointed with God. We say we are ready to turn our hearts over to the Lord and surrender our lives to Him, when really, we don't completely trust Him.

This might be tough to admit, especially for Christians with great faith. But we're human beings, with weaknesses and limitations, and it's pride to think our spiritual life is perfect. We are always in need of greater faith, trust and confidence in God.

Since we have feelings and experiences that aren't always pleasant we shouldn't try to hide this from God in prayer. As we develop the practice of silent prayer in our lives we will grow in faith and learn to trust God more and more. It will become easier as we let our guard down and allow God to love the real us, unpleasant feelings and all. We don't have to wear our false image on our sleeve in prayer. God knows how we *really* feel. We are here to be healed, not to be perfect.

Let's not wait to be in a good mood or have the right feelings or right thoughts before coming to God in prayer. If we did, we would never come! We don't need to change before we receive God's Love, because God's Love is what will change us. This change will occur in the encounter - a gentle, compassionate, safe and peaceful conversation of heart with our Heavenly Father. As we do this more and more, things will start to get better.

We have a God who loves us, who will accept us just the way we are, with all of our humanity, weaknesses and feelings, both good and bad. When we get into the practice of silent prayer, some of those feelings may come up. Let them, and then let them go. Without judgment, give them to God. Over time we will learn which ones are in need of healing and which are distractions. So if thoughts or feelings come to mind during silent prayer, we can simply present them to God and keep our focus on Him.

We need to let go of the "right way" and "wrong way" to pray. Being in a bad mood, but still coming to the Lord faithfully in our silent prayer time, with our bad mood, admitting our bad mood, is holy. Pretending everything is alright when it isn't, is not. God is real, and we need to be real too. The Lord knows us. He knows the real us, and maybe we need to stop thinking we're so terrible because we're not perfect.

God knows our needs

Here's where we begin to pray in a new way. We are so used to asking God for what we want, explaining to Him what we need Him to do for us. Now, in silent prayer, we quietly trust that He knows our needs better than we do.

I can remember one time, someone told me to say this prayer, *"Lord, grant that I may be happy, no matter what."* A beautiful prayer that I tried to say but couldn't. I couldn't get the words on my lips. I was praying for something very specific at the time. I didn't want God to make me happy no matter what. I wanted God to do this, that and the other thing, and then I knew I would be happy.

But think about it, happy is happy. If we're happy, then, what does it really matter what our circumstances are. It's really a great and deeply spiritual prayer to say - with some practice in my case.

We usually don't ask for anything unreasonable in prayer. We think we know what we need. Our prayers make sense to us. They're understandable. They may even be holy and helpful to others. We design a method of praying that supports our good intentions, so that we don't ask God for something He won't give us. Then, when we don't get it, we're a mess. What went wrong? It was a good prayer. We wonder if we prayed "wrong." Or maybe we didn't make clear to God what we were asking. Silent prayer will bring clarity to this confusion and help us to trust God when things don't make sense.

God knows what we don't. He knows what we need better than we do. We can stop playing the game now. We can stop trying to say the right prayer and use the right words and ask for the right things, and just be ourselves, with the Lord. What we say to God is less important than what He says to us, and we can only hear Him, if we're listening.

Being ourselves

God knows who we really are, and who we really want Him to think we are. We may think that we are approaching God in prayer, when really God is the one calling us to pray. It's an invitation that our heart has finally allowed ourselves to receive. Now that we can hear the invitation, it's time for a reply. But the invitation came first. God's Spirit is moving within us, drawing us away from our fears and closer to Love. God doesn't call us to come to Him in prayer as somebody else. He calls *us*.

When my niece was very little, her cousins were playing hide and seek with her. It was her turn to hide. All the adults in the room had ideas for her as to where she should go, but she was very independent and wanted to do it herself. So she just sat down on the floor in the center of the room, where we could all see her, and with a big smile as if she had found the greatest hiding spot ever, covered her face.

When we go into prayer, let me save you the suspense - God sees you! We can cover our eyes if we want, but that only limits *our* vision, not God's.

God knows that relationship with Him is what will make everything new for us. It's not just about who we are, it's about *who God is*. We don't need to worry about putting on a disguise before we come to God in prayer, hoping He won't be able to guess who it is. He knows, and loves us regardless. Let's not allow fear to get in the way.

Let's not be afraid to approach a God who loves us so deeply, who desires so intensely to be loved in return. Let's not be afraid to come to a God who wants so much to be with us that He came to earth and became a human being. Let's not be afraid of a God who would shed every last drop of His blood for us so that we might be saved. God is good. All the time. He is approachable and available.

We come to pray the way we are. With all of our heart, needs, hopes and dreams. With all of our anxieties, *casting our cares upon the Lord for He cares for us (1 Peter 5:7)*. We don't pretend. Not anymore. This is the new way we pray. We believe in a God who already loves us, and understands us. We trust in a God who became one of us. We bring our hearts to Him. Knowing He knows, and knowing He knows that we know, we come, just as we are, and pray.

Chapter 5

A Prayerful Disposition

We come to the Lord, as we come to no other. We can speak with Him openly as a kind friend knowing He's listening and understanding our needs and concerns.

God is our companion for the journey. He's is our confidant, we can tell Him anything, and He won't withdraw His Love. He is approachable, and forgiving.

Therefore, we come into silent prayer with a grateful attitude. God has given us everything. He has given us His Church, His Life, His Death, His Body and Blood, His Holy Spirit dwelling within us, helping us day after day with the graces we need. There is nothing God has withheld from us. He is closer than our own breath, and He is our greatest friend.

But He's also God. As personable and approachable as our Maker is, He is still our Maker and a reverential disposition is required on our part when we enter into prayer. We shouldn't distance ourselves from God in prayer because He's Divine in nature, we should move closer to Him because of it, and as the friend that He is, but we do so with an appreciation and respect of His infinite Goodness.

Humility

"And whoever exalts himself shall be humbled; and whoever humbles himself shall be exalted" (Matthew 23:12.)

We need God, and we live in a world that doesn't think so. A world where God is a great idea but not necessary. A world that tells us God is whoever we want Him to be. A world that creates God, in *our* image, according to our own likes and dislikes. God is fashioned and welcomed in our lives as long as He abides by *our* rules. A world that tells us we're all going to heaven anyway, no matter what we do, because God is love and therefore we don't need to worry about sin or hell. A world that tells us we don't need a Savior. A world that tells us there's no reason to seek Him in any real or meaningful way, especially if it's inconvenient or interferes with our life. So as long as He's the way I believe, it's all good.

This is called relativism, where there's no such thing as absolute truth. What's good for you is good for you, and what's good for me is good for me. We are not talking about what you like to eat or what clothes you wear. We are talking about moral relativism. It says there's really no right or wrong, there's just what you like and don't like, and what I like and don't like. It's an idea that says you go ahead and believe in the God you want to, and I'll believe in the God I want to and both are true. That both are ok.

Here's the thing. There is only one God. God is God. He's the Creator, we're the creature. He came first, we came second. It is not up to us to decide who God is but rather to *discover* who He is. And He provides us the means to do that. It's called prayer. And this is what happens in silent prayer. We seek Him, and we find Him. We let go of our pride and open up our hearts and allow Him to reveal Himself to us.

Only humility can lead us to such knowledge of God. So it's important that we come to prayer with a deep respect for our place in this relationship. As we enter into a deeper and more serious prayer life, we will come to experience God as He actually is, right in our very own heart.

Humility allows us to grow in our prayer life. We will see more clearly how valuable we are. We will start to understand that our worth comes from Him. Our Life comes from Him. It's *all* about Him. And we pray that way - *with* Him.

Openness

We develop new habits when we commit ourselves to a few minutes of quiet time with the Lord. Our thinking will change and we will then enter into prayer time with more and more the right attitude. It will become easier to be spiritually prepared in life.

Our preparation begins with being humble and open to God's grace. We come with an expectant attitude, ready to receive, ready to make contact with the Lord in this special way. In other words, we don't sit down to prayer half aware of what we're doing with an attitude of "ok Lord whatever" watching the minutes pass by so we can get on with our day.

We come, hoping. We bring our desire to God. Maybe we hope He will lift a burden from us that day. Maybe we hope to feel His Love. Maybe we are looking to be strengthen and refreshed by Christ. We come, ready to receive.

We come with faith, believing that God Loves me, that God knows me and knows how I'm feeling today, and that He will help me. We don't say "whatever". We say yes. Yes to God's presence in our lives. Yes to a new life of peace and calm in the midst of the storm. We say yes to the Heart that created ours. We ask and receive, beyond words, simply by being present there, and we trust that God is there too.

Above all we come to be loved by Him. This is a natural human desire, to receive the Love of our Creator, to receive the Love who made us. Every heart longs for this love, whether we admit it or not. This place that only God can fill is built into us, it's part of our nature to want to know God, to love God and to serve God. Many of our problems come from resisting this truth.

We come into silent prayer wanting to receive a divine smile on our life. We come wanting to know a love like no other can give, a love that is not dependent upon circumstances or appearances or situations. A Love that just is. It's wonderful. We don't have to do anything to earn it.

Praying with God

Without realizing it, we are sometimes praying *at* God, probably because He has felt so distant from us. We pray toward Him, in His direction, yes, but we pray as if He's in one place and we're in another. Centering prayer takes us away from this type of thinking. When we grow in our prayer life by taking time to listen to the Lord, we soon discover He's there *with* us in prayer, with us all the time.

This is why we come to silent prayer in the first place. We seek our God's presence. We find it in the quiet of our hearts, and when we do we will grow in His Love for us and see things differently.

We discover that God lives within us. That God resides in the heart He created. That's where He is, inside us. What we are doing in centering prayer is accepting Him as being there. We come to a place in our hearts, and a place in our lives where we sense God is present. He's not somewhere way off in a land far, far away.

"Do not be afraid. Do not be discouraged, for the Lord your God will be with you wherever you go" (Joshua 1:9).

God is here. Now. It may feel like He is far away. It may feel like He doesn't care. It may feel like He has abandoned us. But these are feelings. What we seek in silent prayer is the reality of God's presence in our lives, and so these feelings will change as we experience Him more fully, present to us, as part of our life, not removed from it.

With our whole heart

It's a wonderful irony that God is the whisper within our hearts. The world has us looking just about everywhere else for Him. We've been looking in the wrong places, or perhaps simply in the wrong way.

"For I know the plans I have for you,"
declares the Lord, "plans to prosper
you and not to harm you, plans to give
you hope and a future. Then you will
call on me and come and pray to me,
and I will listen to you. You will seek
me and find me, when you seek me with
all your heart. I will be found by you,"
declares the Lord, "and will bring you
back from captivity" (Jeremiah 29:11-
14).

This scripture is jam packed with good stuff. First we hear God has a plan - a great one - one we can look forward to with hope. What a relief this is. Especially for those of us who don't know what we're doing, it's refreshing to hear that God does.

He has a plan, and we don't just pray to get to the plan, rather, prayer itself is part of the plan. God's plan is to have relationship with us. We can know Him as He really is. We hear in this Scripture that God wants this too! It's not just on our end. This relationship occurs only through a devoted, faithful and consistent prayer life.

God is seeking us out. He's the one calling us to Himself. But a response is required on our part. He tells us in the above scripture exactly what to do. *"Call on me", "come", " pray to me."* He's inviting us. Praying to God is itself, His Will. He tells us not to be afraid, that He has no bad intention, and He tells us clearly He will hear us. *"I will listen to you."* God wants our prayers. We are not bothering Him. He has a plan, and He wants to reveal it to us.

We've sought Him, but how do we find Him? *"You will seek me and find me, when you seek me with all your heart."* All of our heart. Not a corner of it or the surface of it. All of it. God didn't just make a portion of our hearts. He made everything about us, and He loves what He has made.

If we could only accept that God *is* Love, we would accept that we belong to Love. We were made by Love for Love, and Love itself, Loves us.

There is nothing other than Love guiding all of this. There is nothing other than Love permeating our prayer time. Love is the root and reason for it. God just loves us. The amount of energy we use trying to evaluate whether or not that's really true, is exhausting.

We pray *with* God, *in* God. We pray silently with an understanding that there is no separation between us. In contemplative prayer, we just are, and God just is. We are in God and God is in us. We come with thanksgiving, with reverence, expecting, believing, and being open to the healing touch of God's grace in our lives.

Chapter 6

Finding Time

How can we find five to fifteen minutes of our day to give to God? The Creator of time, is worthy of our time. There's so much we take for granted from God, things we just assume will always be there. We forget all that He has provided for us. He has given us life. He made us. We forget that He maintains our existence. Love keeps us going. Literally. God is Love, therefore Love supports our very next breath. We don't live without Him. Yes, we can give Him a few minutes of our day.

Think about the things we find five minutes for and we'd be surprised just how many five minutes there are in the day that we use doing less important things. The amount of time it takes for us to eat a snack, or watch a TV show, or flip through a magazine.

If a friend needed help with something, or someone we love needed advice, we'd give them a few minutes. If the phone rang and the number of somebody we wanted to talk to

69

showed up on the caller I.D., we would answer it.

God's calling

It's for you. Our Lord is on the line. This is what silent prayer is all about. We get in touch with God. We pick up the phone. We answer the call and we listen. We keep our appointment. We show up! We don't wait for time to show up for us. We make it happen. Why? Because it has value for us.

Coming to God in silent prayer, says a lot. Even just that much, just showing up, already speaks volumes. God is thrilled to see us coming. Why? We make time for what's important to us. So He sees that He is important to us. Without any words, we are already pleasing the Lord just by our presence. I would say not only that this makes Him happy, I'd go so far as to say He's ecstatic when we come to sit quietly with Him in prayer, seeking His voice in our lives. He calls out all day long to every human heart to return to Him, to approach Him and be Loved. He wants to spend time with those He has given life to ... and we showed up. We said yes.

Quality, not quantity

"A thousand years in your sight are like a day that has just gone by" (Psalm 90:4). What's a few minutes to God - nothing. What's a few minutes *for* God - everything! We will begin centering prayer just a few minutes a day if we're not used to praying quietly. Eventually, the amount of time may increase, but the most important aspect is that we remain faithful to the practice and do it every day.

It's better to do five minutes every day of the week than to do one hour on only one day of the week. The reason is that we are forming a relationship, and want to stay in close contact. Think of your relatives and friends who you don't see very much. Maybe on a holiday once or twice a year, you spend a good amount of time, a few hours or so with them. Imagine instead if you spoke to them every day, for a much shorter amount of time. It would change the relationship. From once or twice a year, to every day.

It's the quality of time we spend with the Lord that matters, more than the quantity. It's our openness of heart that matters. We could

71

spend an hour in prayer with the door to our heart shut, or two minutes in prayer rolling out the red carpet for the Lord to enter and do whatever He wants with us. In that case, the two minutes would make more of a difference, because we have allowed Love to come in. It is our openness to God and our faithfulness and consistency in prayer that counts more than anything else.

When we refer to God as coming into our hearts, we say it knowing He is already there. It might sound like a contradiction, but it's not. God is everywhere. He lives within us. We just pile a lot of life on top of Him, and cover Him up. In silent prayer, we allow God to show up again, and to enter, healing our "life's stuff", cleaning up our hearts of the past. Then we find Him again, present with us, inside and out.

Time management

Our Lord knows how busy and complicated life can be. He's not indifferent to our struggles and concerns. Jesus understands our humanity and how stressful life is. God became man in the person of Jesus Christ, and our pain and suffering is something He comprehends well.

He also knows that the world we live in doesn't exactly make Him a high priority and this only makes things more difficult for us. He knows your heart is heavy and your life is hard. He has the power to help, but in the absence of prayer we tell Him we don't have time for help. But is that really working out for us?

The irony of silent prayer in our daily lives is that we think we don't have time to do it, yet doing it helps us manage our time. On the surface, maybe the thought of finding fifteen minutes of quiet time in a busy household sounds more like a dream than a prayer. Maybe if we have a job that keeps us occupied day and night, we're too overwhelmed or exhausted to think about praying. Or maybe, there's fifteen minutes in there somewhere and we just haven't looked for it in a serious way. This afternoon I ate a bag of potato chips - there's seven minutes I can't get back. Only we know the degree to which we are willing to make time for God.

Another thing we can do is to ask God to help us find the time. He loves this one. This is a prayer He will always answer yes to. God will work it out. If we are sincere, He will make a way. He will give us an idea, or the grace to get up fifteen minutes earlier. I know, I know, that's a tough one and maybe we've tried it already, but let's try it again, this time with God's help.

The point is, we have to make a move. We have to make time for God. It's not going to just happen, and let's please not wait until we feel like it. It's an act of the will and we can pray regardless of our mood. God will help us find time to pray, but the decision to pray comes from our free will. We choose it. It has to come from us.

The Present Moment

When we think of time, we think of it from our perspective. It costs something. We can't be in two places at once so if we're doing one thing then we're not doing something else. We prioritize and assess our needs and make decisions accordingly, so they fit in the hours of the day. Hopefully, we will soon put silent prayer and our relationship with God high up on that list. But it's our list, and we're limited to time. God isn't.

God is the great *"I AM."* We need to remember this when we pray. We are close to Him, but not equal to Him. He is not limited to time. He's not limited at all. He just "is." When we enter into a deeper relationship with the Lord through centering prayer, we seek Him where He is - here, now. There is no other moment for Him. He exists only in this one. We waste so many moments thinking about other moments that we miss the one that matters. This moment.

For those of us who want to pray quietly this is great news. God will never cancel our appointment with Him. He's always there. He is not constricted to time and place. We can re-schedule if we need to. But it benefits us to try our best to make a commitment to time and place so as to develop a habit of silent prayer. Making it part of the schedule, part of our day, and with practice, part of our lives.

In silent prayer, we give everything to God. By making this practice a daily part of our lives, we accept Him as the center or it all. It's hardly a passive act, as it will change us. We meet God in the depths of our hearts, and as a result are transformed into someone new!

Let's not put it off any longer. Let's *"come and see" (John 1:46)* for ourselves what a life of intimate prayer with God will do for us. Let's open ourselves up to the possibility of inner change. In addition, let's experience what it will do for our relationships, for those in our lives who will also benefit by the new person we've become. Let's consider God's power to change us, to make us new, to transform our hearts through prayer.

Chapter 7

The Basics

Prayer is good. All forms that seek to develop and maintain a relationship with our Heavenly Father through His Son, Jesus Christ is Holy. Vocal prayer is essential to the Christian life, and as followers of Jesus we maintain our friendship with Him through relationship with Him, through conversation with Him. God wants us to talk with Him, to verbalize our concerns and tell Him about our day. God wants us to ask and to receive.

We can pray using words anytime we want. While we're walking around, while we're traveling, while cooking dinner, etc. God is always with us. He can always hear us and we should be encouraged to communicate with Him, and petition God always. *"Pray without ceasing" (1 Thessalonians 5:17).* God is the greatest friend we will ever have, and we should have constant contact with Him.

This book is referring only to one of the ways we stay in contact with God, and it can't be done effectively while walking around or traveling or cooking dinner. We need to pause and catch our breath, or rather catch the breath of The Holy Spirit. We need to put aside the noise of our life. We need to bask in Love for a few minutes and be renewed. We need to listen to what God is saying to our heart. We need to *be still*.

We have some of the basics down already. We'll discuss some more of the practice of silent prayer in this chapter, but let's review some of the key points.

God Loves you. His Love for you has no limit or conditions. He just loves you. It's what He does. It's who He is. You are safe and sound in the Sacred Heart of Jesus Christ.

We say yes to God's invitation to come to Him and we add a certain amount of quiet time to our prayer life. Through this practice of silent prayer, we open up our hearts and let God love us.

We do this by making a choice to set aside a certain amount of dedicated time each day. Starting off simply and understanding it's the quality of the time that matters.

We choose a quiet place. We turn off the noise, the T.V., the computer, the cell phone. We don't "do" anything. We just come.

We ask God to help us find time and a good place to pray in. Even if we have to get up early or go in our car for a few minutes for some peace and quiet, He will help us and that will make it easier.

We're prepared mentally with a right attitude about the process. Grounded in the fact that God is Good and He Loves us, we come before Him in faith, with expectant hope, in a prayerful and reverent manner.

We know it's important to keep our prayer life consistent and remain faithful to our quiet time with God on a daily basis.

We are here to be with God. Showing up is the most lovable thing we can do and God will bless us for it. We know we do this for ourselves, but we are also aware we do it for Him, who wants so much to spend time with us too.

We come as we are! This is the most important part of praying this way. We won't be rejected and we're allowed to be ourselves! God will not withdraw His Love from us. He can't. He would stop being God if He did. He is Love.

We don't have to disguise ourselves. God cannot be deceived. We can't put one over on Him. He already knows the condition of our hearts, so let's try and be as real as we can. He will not reject us. He knows we are wounded and afraid. We can remove the mask we wear in front of the rest of the world. We are sitting with our God now, and we don't have to pretend.

We don't have to go through some check list before we pray, making sure we're perfect in mind and mood before we enter into prayer. We can enter into silent prayer as an absolute emotional mess and God will love us through it.

We understand that we are forming a relationship with God in a new way and it may take time to really trust Him with our heart. But we come anyway.

These are some of the basics. It's also worth mentioning that the best time to spend with the Lord is in the morning. This isn't easy but mornings have a unique advantage in that it sets the tone for the day. We show God we are putting Him first on the agenda and we align our heart with His to receive strength and grace for the coming day. But God will draw us close to Himself at any time, and you and the Lord can work that out. For our purposes here, let's just set up a meeting with Him and keep the appointment, whatever time it is.

It's also worth mentioning that we don't have to feel like praying in order to pray. There are going to be plenty of times when we will feel like "skipping it" today. This is normal but we need to recognize the signs so as to prevent this from happening. Certain things, like not planning ahead, or an unwillingness to adjust certain activities can make it easy for us to fall into a rut and eventually stop silent prayer altogether.

Or maybe after a few weeks or months we feel like we've gotten enough out of silent prayer and can stop now. This is never the case. We are never done with prayer. We are never done with our relationship to God. It will even carry over into Heaven. So let's take the time to get to know God now, since the plan is to spend eternity with Him anyway. God's love for us never ends, and our desire to know His love will never end either.

It can't be emphasized enough, we have to make silent prayer a daily practice for it to make a difference in our spiritual life. As time goes on we will be looking forward to it, excited about our personal and spiritual growth. But if you're not in that kind of a mood right now the invitation is still there, and we are still called to come. It's not a magic pill or a quick solution to a problem. It's a way of life, a way of prayer, a way to grow in Love, and live in Love. It takes time and commitment, and God's grace.

For Starters

For some of us, this may be the first time we are praying silently and it may take some getting used to. So if you're used to saying vocal prayers, begin with that. If you're used to reading Scripture in prayer, then start there. Read a passage, and then quietly reflect on it. Begin by thanking God and praising Him. Saying something as simple as "Thank you Lord for loving me" or "thank you for this time together" or simply "Praise you Jesus" can really lifts our spirits and get the ball rolling in the right direction.

Don't get too caught up with "do's" and "don'ts" when it comes to silent prayer. This isn't a test. You're not going to get graded. You're not going to fail. Just ask God for the grace to let Him into your heart.

Start off praying with words at first if that helps. Be honest with Him. Tell Him that you want to trust Him with your heart but you don't know how. Tell Him you're in need of something more but you don't know what it is. Tell Him about the prayer you're hoping He will answer and your disappointment about the one

He didn't. Tell Him you're angry. Tell Him you are having trouble forgiving. Tell Him you don't understand His Will sometimes. Tell Him your concerns and fears. But also tell Him you love Him, and that you want to be healed. Tell Him you're sorry. Tell Him everything. Whatever it is. Then sit there, quietly, for a few minutes, and get up and go about your day, *with* God.

Remember, all prayer is good and as long as we are on the way to a relationship with God, that's what matters most. We are on our way to knowing God's infinite Love for us in a way that is new and life-changing, and silent prayer is a beautiful way to get there.

Letting Go

We don't, however, get there on our own. We need God to help us pray. We need God for everything. We can't take our next breath without Him and we certainly can't experience His loving presence in our lives without Him. We need His grace. He calls us to Himself and He's the one who brings us to Himself.

The Holy Spirit guides us in silent prayer. He is Love and knows we need to be Loved. The Spirit of Christ leads us and we follow. We give Him permission to Love us through our time together.

When we try to guide God through our prayer time we get nowhere. We need to surrender control and keep it simple. We are here to be loved, and to be transformed by this Love. We here to find rest for our souls. We're here to be with God. We're just here. We got an invitation and we showed up. God will do the rest.

Even when we quiet the noise around us, there may still be some noise within us. We have things on our mind, concerns come up and of course we'll get distracted. This is all to be expected. We're human. We're not robots. Everything about us comes into prayer with us. Life tags along. But we will learn to let go of these things as we make progress in silent prayer. We will be able to give them to God and focus on God. Thoughts and feelings will arise and without any judgment we will let them go. We will learn not to use up this precious time with God by diving into every unspoken thought or worry that comes to mind, or we would forget all about The Lord. However, certain things may need attention.

When we come to silent prayer, we come with a lot of "stuff." We're human and we have baggage that we haven't unpacked yet. There are many benefits to silent prayer that remain to be discussed but among them is healing of the pain of our past.

The past gets in the way of our present, and the Lord doesn't want anything to come between us and Him. He wants us to be made new! *"I will give you a new heart, and put a new spirit in you" (Ezekiel 36:26).* This is what we receive as a result of silent prayer. God's healing touch. Something that no one else can give us. And this inner healing is worth our time.

We come as we are, and while we're there if certain painful memories or feelings arise we simply present them to God. I like to imagine I'm placing these things at the foot of the Cross, leaving it to Jesus to take care of. And He does. Let's not allow our feelings to guide us in silent prayer. Let's allow God to.

Chapter 8

"Lord, Teach Us To Pray"

"But when you pray, go to your inner room, close the door, and pray to your Father in secret. And your Father who sees in secret will repay you" (Matthew 6:6).

"He said to them, 'Come away by yourselves to a deserted place and rest a while.' People were coming and going in great numbers, and they had no opportunity even to eat. So they went off in the boat by themselves to a deserted place" (Mark 6:31-32).

"Rising very early before dawn, He left and went off to a deserted place, where He prayed" (Mark 1:35).

"But He would withdraw to deserted places to pray" (Luke 5:16).

"In those days, He departed to the mountain to pray, and He spent the night in prayer to God. When day came, He called His disciples to Himself" (Luke 6:12-13).

"Then they came to a place named Gethsemane, and He said to His disciples, 'Sit here while I pray" (Mark 14:32).

"He was praying in a certain place, and when He had finished, one of His disciples said to Him, 'Lord, teach us to pray'" (Luke 11:1).

Jesus practiced silent prayer. Maybe when you saw the title of this chapter you were expecting to hear *The Our Father* - the greatest prayer of all. We see in these Scriptures Jesus practicing what He preaches to us. He leads us by word, and by example. He is doing what He calls us to do. Time and again, Jesus withdrew to a quiet place to pray. It didn't just happen.

Our Lord doesn't play games with us and the Gospel passages are not mistakes. This is silent prayer. It's Biblical. We have both encouragement and instruction from God to practice quiet, contemplative, meditative, silent prayer. To commune with God one on one, in a place without distractions. Now, I love the one where Jesus, *"spent the night in prayer"* and *"When day came."* That's no five minutes, but I'd say He was advanced.

There are many reasons to practice silent prayer, but this one is the greatest - because Jesus did.

Union with God

What happens when we go off to be with God alone? What is it that the soul is really seeking? God is our center, and when we meet at the center, we unite. Our heart meets His Heart. We are ultimately seeking oneness. To be in harmony with God.

"Why did God make you? God made me to know Him, to love Him, and to serve Him in this world, and to be happy with Him forever in Heaven" (Baltimore Catechism No. 1).

I have always thought this to be the perfect answer to the question every human heart has, whether we ask it or not. Always I am struck by the proper order of the answer. First - *God made me to know Him.* That's it! That's everything. The answer could actually stop there because when we know God, we will love God. That's just what happens when we encounter Him, who is Love itself. And when we love God, we'll want to serve Him.

This service, love of God and neighbor, is what brings us true joy and fulfillment leading to a happiness that will last forever in Heaven. But it all starts with *knowing* God. And we come to know Him through prayer. Everything flows from that. Knowledge of God is what life itself is about, and it's what we seek, and find, in silent prayer.

God gave all

"For God so loved the world that He gave His one and only Son, that whoever believes in Him shall not perish but have eternal life" (John 3:16).

God created us for Himself. No, he's not a narcissist. He's Love and perfect joy, and wants everyone to know this love and joy too. God wasn't lonely when He created us. He was sharing. He didn't "have to" create us. He didn't need us to exist. He *wanted* us to exist! He wasn't unfulfilled seeking something outside of Himself. He wanted us to share in His fulfillment. God was completely Happy in His own relationship as Father, Son, and Holy Spirit. But Love gives, and so He gave. He gave us life. He gave us Himself. He sent His Son and His Spirit. He wants us to know His joy.

How can that be? Because Love can't be divided. God can't split Himself up in pieces. When God shares, it's not like when we do. He doesn't keep some for Himself. He can't. Because *He* is what He's giving us. He's giving us Himself, totally. There is no such thing as God loving us "a little bit". Love is complete. It is full in and of itself. Each of us gets the whole pie.

So Jesus not only teaches us how to pray, He teaches us how to live, by also giving totally and completely of ourselves too. To be givers, not thinking of self. We can't know what that's like without God showing us. God became man, took on human flesh, and showed us what Love really looks like.

In the person of Jesus Christ, God teaches us what true Love is. Through His words and His examples, He reveals to us what will bring us a new life! This is why He came. *"I came that they may have life and have it abundantly" (John 10:10).* In silent prayer we seek this abundant spiritual life in Christ.

Chapter 9

Beyond Words

Some things are beyond words including our prayers. Sometimes we just don't know what to say. Life can feel overwhelming at times and certain situations are just too complicated to explain. Words may fail us, but God won't. He understands our heart. We can enter into silent prayer, look up at the Lord, and sigh, and He will know what we are trying to say.

God understands our sigh. He knows everything it entails. He receives the breath within it and all of the unspoken pleas throughout it. He knows what our heart is saying, and what it isn't. What's so wonderful about silent prayer, is that God doesn't *need* our words. Sometimes the sigh is more appropriate. It takes less time and communicates much more. It's something between you and God alone. He knows, and you know He knows. Then you sit there, and let Him love you.

This is the heart of centering prayer. We spend some time *with* God. We don't *do*. We don't *say.* We don't *think*. We rest in His Love.

This takes some getting used to because there's no cause and effect. We don't normally function this way. We live in a world where we have to earn our share, we have to work, we have to try. In our daily lives an effort is required of us in order to achieve and it's exhausting. God however, doesn't work that way and He wants to show us a whole new world, one where things are freely given.

In centering prayer, we don't "*have to.*" We can take a break from pretending that we aren't in desperate need of God's grace in our lives. We can let go of our pride. We can let go of our controlling nature. We can stop *trying*. We don't have to do anything to be loved. Most of the unrest in our soul is because we try to earn God's love, something that is completely unnatural to God and inconsistent with who He is. He is Love, and He just Loves. You can't work for it. Even if you tried you wouldn't get any more Love than He already has for you right now.

Seek first the Kingdom

"But seek first the kingdom of God and his righteousness, and all these things will be given to you as well" (Matthew 6:33).

We pray for a reason, with a purpose, and when that purpose is centered on Jesus Christ, everything else falls into place. This is a spiritual truth. It's the *"everything else"* we're interested in at first, but as we grow in silent prayer, it's Jesus we will want. He's the reason we will come.

At first we may have other reasons, but it's holy to desire what is holy. If we desire to receive peace, strength, grace, truth, healing, improved relationships with others, and above all to feel loved in prayer, then this is all good. We come seeking for ourselves in silent prayer, but what we seek is not selfish. We want the gifts of God. Soon we will just want God, understanding that His gifts are wrapped up in Him, one and the same.

God wants us to receive the fruits of silent prayer and be transformed into a new and joyful creation. But we have to be able to recognize the difference between the what and the who in our approach to prayer. The giver comes first, before the gifts can. Jesus gives the blessings and all of our heart and all of our thoughts need to be rooted in Him. This is why in silent prayer we aim to quietly let everything else go, so we can attach ourselves to Christ. When we receive Him, we receive everything.

"Ask and it will be given to you. Seek and you will find. Knock and the door will be opened to you" (Matthew 7:7). In centering prayer, we're doing more than asking God for a favor or handing Him a petition list. We're looking for Him. Jesus is the one we seek and He wants us to seek Him. In the above scripture He tells us to seek Him and assures us that if we do - *if* we do - that we will find Him.

This has nothing to do with the amount of time we pray, but rather our openness of heart. It's proportional. If we seek God a little bit, we're going to find God a little bit. But if we seek God with all of our heart we will find answers to questions we didn't even know we had.

We will encounter a love that has no limit, and when we find this, our lives will change, because *we* will change. This Love becomes part of us and so now wherever we go, we can bring it into the world.

Christ as our center

Christ *is* our center. We don't use Jesus in centering prayer to get what we want. He *is* what we want. He is the center of *all* life, and therefore the center of ours. Christ is the center of everything. In silent prayer we come to a deeper understanding of how we are rooted in Christ Jesus.

In the core of our hearts, which God created, we find Christ in a new way. It's where He lives. He belongs there. When we see God in the world, through the kind, holy and unselfish acts of others, it is with the eyes of our heart that we see it. We recognize what is good because we now recognize Goodness within us. He is our Creator, our Savior, and our Life. He's not confined to a space, but there is something about the heart. More accurately, there is something about Christ's heart, that is beyond words.

God's Will

When we come to know God in prayer, we will fall in Love with Him, and as a result we will want to serve Him. We will want to *love others as He has loved us* (John 13:34). But how? God has a plan for our lives, and through silent prayer we can discover what it is as the Lord speaks to our hearts. It probably won't be revealed all at once but God will guide our steps. The spiritual ears of our heart will come to recognize The Good shepherd's voice.

Every day we come to prayer, we will become more open to the actions of The Holy Spirit in our lives. As we grow in our prayer life, we will be better able to see what Love wants from us. Through prayer, we will acquire the grace to let Love, love us, and understand what He wants is for us to bring His Love to others. We will be better able to seek His Will for us, to grow in the knowledge of how and in what capacity He would like us to serve Him. And we will receive the grace to do it.

Silent prayer offers us the opportunity to discern and to respond to God's call, regardless of what it is. Often, we can get so caught up in wanting to know God's Will for our entire life, that we forget He has a will for our daily life. Maybe today He wants us to forgive someone. I know it might not sound as grand as preaching to the masses, or forming your own charity organization, but if it's God's will for us then that's what we're called to do.

Maybe He wants us to smile at everyone we meet today, radiating His love to others. Maybe He wants us to add sixty seconds to our silent prayer time with Him each day. After all, God can do more in one minute, than we could in a lifetime. Perhaps He's calling us to be a little more grateful for the people in our lives and all the blessings we have and appreciate the gifts He gives us.

Maybe God's will isn't as complicated as we make it to be sometimes. Yes, there's a big picture and I believe a bigger purpose for our lives in which God has a big plan, but let's not forget, *"Rejoice always, pray continually, and give thanks in all circumstances. For this is God's will for you in Christ Jesus"* (1 *Thessalonians 5:16-18).* Let's strive to achieve this, and God will take care of everything else.

Silent prayer both reveals and prepares us to live the Christian life more fully. We have nothing to fear. God's will is always good, and it will bring us true inner peace. We just need to listen in order to hear. We need to follow the voice of our Shepherd and be led by His Spirit, as we walk the path He has laid out for us.

We are called by God to fulfill His purpose for our lives, not someone else's. We need to be patient with ourselves as He guides our steps in the right direction. We need to pray over it. We need to come to the quiet.

"What eye has not seen, and ear has not heard, and what has not entered the human heart, what God has prepared for those who love him" (1 Corinthians 2:9.) God has something pretty amazing in store for us, beyond our imagination. He has a plan, and we're part of it. When we come to pray quietly before the Lord, we find rest because we are sitting with the One who has everything under control.

Chapter 10

The Blessings

The blessings we receive as a result of practicing Christian silent prayer are too many to list. We're trying to describe something here that can't be explained and the fruits of it can barely be explained either, but we'll touch on a few of them. I'll say one thing for sure, the benefits are eternal.

Both the purpose and the primary benefit of silent prayer is that we grow in holiness. This is what every human person is called to - to be more like Christ. This is the ultimate goal of centering prayer. To achieve a union with God, that brings His Love back to earth once again. Bringing what is holy and good and right into a world that can be godless and cruel.

There are blessings we receive in silent prayer that are wonderful, that make us brand new and make our lives better. These are the ones that keep us coming back, and there are even more blessings waiting for us. But we don't receive the fruits of centering prayer just for ourselves. We receive them to be shared with others. The blessings we receive prepare us to follow Jesus and to love one another as He loves us. Ultimately, the blessings we receive in our own personal prayer life belong to the entire Body of Christ.

Peace

"Peace I leave with you. My peace I give you. I do not give to you as the world gives. Do not let your hearts be troubled, and do not be afraid" (John 14:27).

Jesus wants us to have peace, and He knows the world can't give it to us. Perhaps we're in a place right now in our lives where we know it too. We've looked to the world for answers but have come up empty. We've sought the world's version of inner peace, and God wasn't there.

The world thinks peace comes from the outside in. In silent prayer we discover the truth. Peace comes from the inside out. The Kingdom of God is within us. Christ lives in our heart. He's there now. The peace Jesus has waiting for us will change our lives, forever. It's a benefit of silent prayer that is well worth our time.

<u>Healing</u>

As mentioned earlier, painful memories or past hurts may come up when we turn the noise down in prayer. The heart is a sacred place, and we guard it well. But when we pray it's important to remember that we have a God who has a heart too and we can let that guard down.

The Heart of Jesus is a safe place. Our hearts are in good hands when we give them to Him. The One who created the human heart knows it well. Our Lord knows what our hearts need, and He also knows what it needs to get rid of. These things deep within us will surface in prayer, but the living God, who we encounter in silent prayer, will heal us.

When we come into silent prayer, we bring all of our wounds with us. We can see in Scripture that Jesus was a Healer, and we trust in His Healing Love. He wants to set us free. Matters of the heart are too complicated for us to handle. We need God's healing touch. We need God to repair us, to soothe us, to patch us up. Inner healing is a life-changing blessing that can come through silent prayer.

Joy

"Do not grieve, for the joy of the Lord is your strength" (Nehemiah 8:10). Joy is not necessarily a feeling, but a contentment that fills us with hope.

In silent prayer we encounter Christ and we are comforted and strengthened by His presence. We don't have to go looking for joy, we just have to go looking for Christ, and He will fill us with good things, even during times of trial.

Joy is a gift from God. Like all of God's gifts it's a grace freely given, not something we can earn. It may take time to recognize joy. We are so used to seeing things a certain way and expecting to feel things a certain way. We are so used to looking for happiness from the world that we might overlook joy from God.

Joy is deeply spiritual. We're at peace, and others can sense it. God is both the Giver and the Gift. In silent prayer we come to know the Giver in a more personal way and His joy is both a blessing we receive in silent prayer, and a way of attracting others to Him.

Grace

Everything we are talking about in this book is grace. We need God's help and we can't merit it. We can't earn it. It's free. God gives us special graces as we go through life. We humbly admit we need His assistance in life, that we can't do it on our own.

His grace works along the natural and is available in the present moment. Have you ever looked back on a certain event in your life, a difficult time you made it through, and thought "how did I ever do that?" or "I don't think I could ever do that again." Well those were moments where you had the grace you needed at the time.

God gives us what we need, when we need it. We have the graces we need right now to do what we're doing right now. Tomorrow we may need His help in another way, and He will provide it. He gives us the ability to do what we are called to do, and one thing I can promise you is that God will always, always, always give us the graces we need to do His will. Let's not be proud and push God's grace out of our life, thinking we can go at it alone. Let's instead rejoice that He helps us along the way.

Better relationships

The practice of silent prayer will also improve our personal life also. As we change, we will carry that change into every aspect of our daily lives and it will end up benefiting everyone around us.

Having encountered Love Himself, we will become more loving. We will become calmer, more still, and radiate more peace in our lives and in our relationships with others. People will notice a change in us, however small at first, and God will use us to bring His love into a broken world.

Silent prayer never leads to selfishness. Even though we look inward we don't stay there. When done properly we are moved out of our ego and into Love. Love never seeks for itself, it always gives more Love, and our family and friends will come to appreciate that we are practicing silent prayer. We will change and find peace in our lives, and then be able to bring that peace into their lives as well.

The Truth

"And you will know the truth, and the truth will set you free" (John 8:32). The benefits we receive in silent prayer aren't only of the heart. The way we think will change too. We will see things in a new way with a new attitude. Our minds will be renewed as well.

When we spend time with the Lord frequently in prayer, we will come to know Him better. We will learn more about Him. Our life will become more prayerful. We'll read more scripture, and meditate on His word more often. We will understand His message better when we combine it with His presence in our hearts.

We will now *"have the mind of Christ" (1 Cor 2:16)* as we grow deeper in faith. Truth will be revealed to us. The truth about God and the truth about ourselves, that we are fully loved by our Heavenly Father. This truth will bring us what we've been seeking and our lives will change for the better. We will no longer *"conform to the pattern of this world, but be transformed by the renewing of our mind" (Romans 12:2).*

It's worth it

Finally, we are made new through silent prayer. We will enjoy a close friendship with the Lord, an intimacy with God, a newfound trust in our Creator. We will be happier than we ever realized we could be. Our lives will now have a meaning and a purpose that we didn't know or understand before.

Beyond words, beyond emotions, in the serenity of the Heart of Jesus we come. We empty our minds and concentrate on Him. We look at Him, and He looks back. In the quiet of our soul, we become still. And we find God, waiting for us.

"I have called you by name. You are mine" (Isaiah 43:1). Our Heavenly Father knows us. He is approachable, and His Spirit will gently guide our steps. He loves us. He already knows us in a personal way, and wants us to know Him too.

Now that we have completed this book, let's renew our commitment to deepen our spiritual life through prayer. Let's walk with Christ on the path to a new life. Let's open our hearts to an actual relationship with God. A life changing, living, breathing relationship with our Creator, who in His Love and Mercy desires to heal us, help us and make us whole.

How can we find five minutes a day to be with the Lord? How can we *not*. All we need to do is *"come"* and spend some time with Him, in a quiet place, and our Lord, who alone knows what we need, will always be there.

May He Bless you on your journey and give you His peace. May you know The Heart of Christ, in a *New Way, Today*.

"Come to Me, all you who are weary and burdened,

and I will give you rest."

Site Information

Join us online for more inspirational Scripture reflections and prayers.

Website:
http://www.newwaytoday.net

Social Media:
www.facebook.com/NewWayToday
www.pinterest.com/NewWayToday
www.twitter.com/NewWay_Today

Other Books:

A New You! Letting Go of the Past, Trusting God with our Future.

Strength For The Weary, Finding Grace in Times of Trial.

Prayers For A New Way. A Prayer Book for the Heart.

New Way Today's Inspirational Reflections for the Soul.

Visit New Way Today's Book Page for more.

And if you found this book helpful in your prayer life and believe it might help others, please consider an online review. Thank you.

May God Bless you and everyone near and dear to you!

35403261R00068

Made in the USA
Middletown, DE
05 February 2019